Off the Shelf

Off the Shelf

An Introduction to the School Library

Eric Williams

Drawings by Roy Schofield

Edward Arnold

© Eric Williams 1979

First published 1979
by Edward Arnold (Publishers) Ltd
41 Bedford Square London WC1B 3DQ

Edward Arnold (Australia) Pty Ltd
80 Waverley Road, Caulfield East
Victoria 3145, Australia

Reprinted 1979, 1981, 1983, 1987

ISBN 0 7131 0307 8

Acknowledgements
The Publisher's thanks are due to A & C Black for
permission to reproduce material from *Stars and Space* by
Patrick Moore. The material on pp. 74-5 is Crown
Copyright, reproduced by kind permission of the Director
Institute of Geological Sciences, London SW7.

Set in 9 on 10 pt Plantin
Made and printed in Great Britain
by Butler & Tanner Ltd, Frome and London

Contents

Foreword

This book is intended for use in the first years of secondary school by the teacher or librarian when introducing pupils to the school library and training them in its use. The book is divided into two sections. The first, 'Introducing the Library', is intended for the teacher to use with a class when explaining the layout of the library and its methods of classification; this section also provides introductory exercises whose aim is to help pupils understand such topics as alphabetical order, referring to encyclopedias and dictionaries, the use of the contents and index of a book when looking for information, the Dewey Decimal System, and the uses and arrangement of the library catalogue. Further practice in referring to encyclopedias and non-fiction for information is provided by the second section of this book, 'Library Assignments'; these assignments are arranged in order of difficulty, so that individual pupils may be given appropriate research tasks. The notes written in answer to the more detailed assignments in the final chapter can be used as the basis for project work on the topics selected. It will be appreciated however that the resources of the school library may not contain the answers to every question in the research assignments in this book: their usefulness lies in framing questions that the pupils can use as guidelines when finding out about the topics selected. These questions can therefore be used as a formula for research: in trying to find the answers to them pupils will probably become interested in other aspects of the topic, and they should be encouraged to pursue these interests in their reading and in their written reports. However, although the questions can thus be seen as starting-points only, if the answer to any of them is not contained in the books on the non-fiction shelves of the school library, the pupils could usefully be asked to consider how they intend to find out this information. A list of further topics and their Dewey reference numbers is given at the end of the book, together with the names of some popular authors of fiction. The pupils can refer to these lists when using the library for themselves.

Section One: Introducing the Library

I Layout–Classification: Fiction, non-fiction, general reference

1   Imagine you are the manager of a new supermarket: it's going to open on Monday next. The shelves in your stores are crammed with boxes full of goods to be sold in your shop when it opens. Tomorrow your staff will begin work taking them from the stores and stocking the shelves in the shop. Before then you have to decide on the layout of your shop, so that your assistants know where to put everything.

On the next page is a plan of your shop, showing the entrances, stores, checkouts (where your customers will pay for what they take from the shelves), the delicatessen counter (where they will buy cold meats, etc.), the frozen foods cabinet, and your office. The plan also shows where your display shelving is, but no details of what is to go on the shelves.

The shelving is shown on the sketch like this:

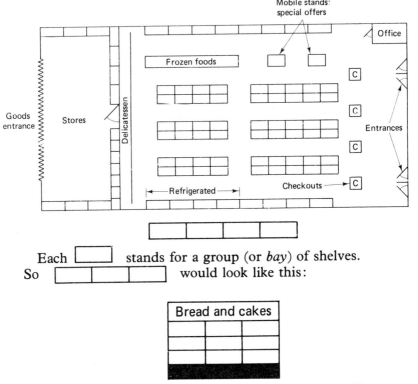

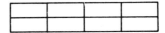

Each ⬚ stands for a group (or *bay*) of shelves.
So ⬚⬚⬚ would look like this:

Bread and cakes		

This shelving is single-sided, perhaps fixed to the wall.
A lot of the shelving in the shop is shown like this:

This means there are bays of shelves on both sides of each unit.
Some of these double-sided units have four bays of shelves on
each side, while others have five. These double-sided units are
not fixed to the wall, but are free-standing.

Draw a larger copy of the plan of your shop shown above.
Add the labels (*frozen foods, delicatessen, mobile stands: special
offers, checkouts, office, entrances,* etc.) and make sure that you have
drawn all the units of display shelving, marking each bay of shelves.

2 Now you will have to work out which further labels must
be added, so that your assistants will know where to put everything
they take from the stores, and so that your customers will be able
to find their way around your shop easily.

a) Before you start to work out where everything must go, make a list of some of the items you are going to sell. Make your list in alphabetical order. The list has been started for you:

a—apples
b—bread
c—cabbage
d—dog foods
e—eggs
f—frozen peas
g—grapefruit
h—hair lacquer
i—ice cream
j—jams
k—kitchen rolls
l—lemons
m—matches
n—nuts
o—oranges
p—potatoes
q/r—ravioli
s—sausages
t—tissues
u/v/w/x/y/z—washing-powder

b) Even though your list will not contain everything that your shop will be selling, there must be enough items for you to realize that you are going to have to put them into groups— otherwise there will be so many labels that it will take your staff far too long to find their way around! Which labels will you give for

    i) cornflakes, porridge, puffed wheat, weetabix
    ii) baked beans, tinned tomatoes, tinned peas, tinned carrots
    iii) cabbage, bananas, oranges, potatoes, cauliflower, carrots
    iv) soap, washing powder, detergents, toothpaste?

Look at the items in your list: which further labels will you need in order to put them into groups?

c) Having decided how you are going to divide up (or *classify*) all the various items your shop will have for sale, add labels to show where each group (or *class*) of goods can be found.

d) When you have finished, compare your plan with your neighbour's. Have you included enough labels for your

customers to be able to find their way around your shop easily?
Which plan is the better—and why?

3   Now imagine you are a librarian. How will you group (or
classify) the thousands of books in your library so that people can
find them easily?

First draw a plan of your school library. Show on your plan:

—the main entrance
—the Library Office/Store
—the Issue Desk or Counter (where you take books you wish
   to borrow or return)
—the Periodicals rack (where magazines and newspapers are
   kept)
—the positions of the bookstacks. Show these in the same way
   as you marked the units of display shelving in the supermarket.

Thus a bookstack fixed against the wall looking like this

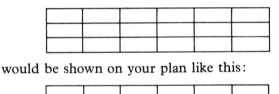

would be shown on your plan like this:

and a free-standing double-sided bookstack like this

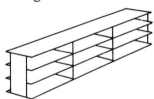

would be shown on your plan like this:

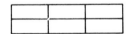

It ought to be possible for you to divide the bookstacks in your
library into three main groups:

Fiction	stories that can be borrowed from the library
Non-Fiction	information books on factual topics (e.g. astronomy, football) that can be borrowed from the library
General Reference	dictionaries, encyclopedias, etc. that cannot be borrowed from the library.

Add these three labels to your library plan.

4   Imagine that the books listed below have just arrived from your bookseller. Say to which area you think each title belongs— *Fiction*, *Non-Fiction* or *General Reference*.

Concise Oxford Dictionary

The Life of Florence Nightingale

Snakes

Ten Western Stories

Chambers Encyclopedia

Gardening For All

Stars and Planets

Fly Fishing For Beginners

The Oxford Atlas

Black Beauty

A Book of Chemistry Experiments

A Journey Through Africa

Treasure Island

Europe in the 18th Century

The Guinness Book of Records

Teach Yourself Chess

Man With A Sword

Liverpool Street Directory

2 Alphabetical Order: Arrangement of the fiction section

Clearly, to avoid confusion, there must be some system of arranging books on the library shelves—just as there is for groceries in a supermarket.

1 The books in the *Fiction* section are arranged in *alphabetical order*. What does this mean? Look at their spines (the edges of the books facing you as you look at them on the shelves) and see how the fiction books are arranged in one of the fiction bays. On each book's spine you will see

its *title* (the name of the story), e.g. *Treasure Island*

its *author* (the name of the person who wrote the story— Robert Louis Stevenson)

and its *publisher* (the firm who prepared the book for sale), e.g. Collins.

Are the books in the Fiction section arranged alphabetically according to their publishers (e.g. all the books published by Arnold coming before those published by Collins), or according to their titles (e.g. *Black Beauty* coming before *Viking's Dawn*), or according to their authors (e.g. Anna Sewell coming before

Henry Treece)? Find out by looking at the books on the shelves in one of the bays of your library's fiction section.

2 Alphabetical order does not just refer to the first letter of each item

apples bananas cabbages

When there is more than one item beginning with the same letter, to group all the items in alphabetical order means arranging them in alphabetical order according to their second letters, and then third, and so on. Look at this list, and see how the items in it are arranged alphabetically:

piano
picnic
picture
pie
pier
pig
pigeon
pillar
pillow
pin
pirate
plank
plastic
plate
plough
plum
poem
poker
police
polish
pony
post
potter
poultry

Complete this list by putting the following words into alphabetical order

present prairie publisher psychologist puzzle
professor projector prescription propeller pyramid
pump public pyjamas pulley prow pylon prune

Where would you add the following items to this list?

person   pocket   pickle   pipe   putty   piston   pip   piglet

3   Put these stories into their correct order for the Fiction section of your library:

Author	Title
Leon Garfield	*Smith*
C. S. Lewis	*The Lion, the Witch and the Wardrobe*
Gerald Raftery	*Snow Cloud, Stallion*
Robert A. Heinlein	*Citizen of the Galaxy*
Arthur C. Clarke	*2001: A Space Odyssey*
Hugh Lofting	*The Story of Doctor Dolittle*
Phillipa Pearce	*A Dog So Small*
Penelope Lively	*The Wild Hunt of Hagworthy*
Andre Norton	*Plague Ship*
John Christopher	*Beyond the Burning Lands*
Patricia Wrightson	*I Own the Racecourse!*
Ursula LeGuin	*A Wizard of Earthsea*
Alan Garner	*Elidor*
Hilda Lewis	*The Ship That Flew*
Meindert Dejong	*The House of Sixty Fathers*
K. M. Peyton	*Flambards*
Barbara Willard	*The Sprig of Broom*
J. Meade Falkner	*Moonfleet*
Peter Dickinson	*Heartsease*
Nina Bawden	*A Handful Of Thieves*
David Line	*Run For Your Life*
Ivan Southall	*Ash Road*

You should have arranged these books in alphabetical order according to their authors. Thus Alan Garner comes after Leon Garfield. How did you decide the order of C. S. Lewis and Hilda Lewis?

4   a)   Arrange these authors into alphabetical order:

Charles Dickens	Rosemary Sutcliff
Joan Aiken	Henry Treece
Noel Streatfeild	William Mayne
Jack London	Roland Welch
Geoffrey Trease	John Masefield

b)   Now find the titles of stories by these authors that are on the shelves of the fiction section of your library.

c)   Make a list in alphabetical order of all the titles of stories you have found for these authors. Leave out *The* or *A* or *An* at the beginning of a title when working out this order—thus for Penelope Lively the list of titles would be

> *Astercote*
> The *Driftway*
> The *Ghost of Thomas Kempe*
> The *Whispering Knights*
> The *Wild Hunt of Hagworthy*

and for C. S. Lewis

> The *Last Battle*
> The *Lion, the Witch and the Wardrobe*
> The *Magician's Nephew*
> *Prince Caspian*
> The *Voyage of the Dawn Treader*

Now make your lists of titles in the same way.

d) A telephone directory is printed alphabetically also. Which books in the *General Reference* section of your library are arranged aphabetically?

3 General Reference Section: Encyclopedias

I a) In the *General Reference* section of the library you will find both dictionaries and encyclopedias. What is the difference between a dictionary and an encyclopedia?

b) Reference books are not read from cover to cover, but are *referred* to so that the reader can find the answer to a specific question: if you want to find out the date of the Battle of Trafalgar, for example, you are likely to find this information more quickly by looking in an encyclopedia in the General Reference section of the library than by looking through all the books in the history section. Notice where the General Reference section of your library is situated: reference books are often to be found near the door so that it is easy to get to them. Why are they not available for people to borrow?

c) What other kinds of books are kept in the General Reference section of your library in addition to encyclopedias and dictionaries? Make a list of them.

d) Sometimes reference books are published in more than one volume. Most encyclopedias have more than one volume. How many volumes are there in each of the encyclopedias in your library?

2   There are so many entries in the London Telephone Directory that it is published in four volumes, which are arranged alphabetically. The first volume contains the names and telephone numbers of subscribers from A to D, the second from E to K, the third from L to R, the fourth from S to Z. So if you want to find the telephone number of the BBC you must look in the first volume, and if you want to phone someone whose surname is Green you have to look in the second volume. In which volume will you find the telephone number of

   i) John Smith
   ii) Edward Arnold, Ltd.
   iii) Harrods
   iv) Thames Television
   v) The National Theatre?

3   a)   Similarly, in an encyclopedia of more than one volume the key letters on the spine of each volume show the first 1, 2 or 3 letters of the first and last subjects dealt with in that volume. In the *Children's Britannica* the full name of the first and last subject is shown on the spine of each volume:

1	2	3	4	5	6	7	8	9	10
Abbey to Arabs	Aran to Bee	Beech to Building	Bulbs to Chub	Church to Czech	Dacca to Environ	Epic to Furs	Galon to Hedin	Helen to Ivy	Jackal to Lomond

11	12	13	14	15	16	17	18	19	20
London to Moss	Moth to Oyster	Pacific to Pond	Pony to Rhyme	Rile to Sedge	Seed to Star	Starch to Toys	Tracks to Walls	Walnut to Zurich	Index and Atlas

b)   In which volume will you find information about

   i) France
   ii) Japan
   iii) Scotland
   iv) Wales
   v) Denmark
   vi) Barbados
   vii) Rome
   viii) Paris
   ix) Moscow
   x) New York?

If your library has the *Oxford Junior Encyclopedia* you will find that its volumes are arranged in a different way: how?

4   See how quickly you can find the answers to this quiz by referring to the encyclopedias in your library. Look up the subject printed in italics (e.g. *Belgium*) at the beginning of each question to find the answer.

1   *Belgium*
   i) What is the capital of Belgium?
   ii) Which is the chief port?
   iii) How many languages are spoken in this country? What are they?

2   *Frogs*
   i) How can you tell the difference between a frog and a toad?
   ii) How do frogs feed?
   iii) How many stages of development are there in a frog's life?

3   *Dolphins*
   i) To which class of animal does the dolphin belong?
   ii) What distinguishes dolphins from porpoises?

4   *Cats*
   i) Cats are divided into two main groups of breed. What are they?
   ii) Why is the Manx cat different from other cats?
   iii) What was the name of the Egyptian goddess with the head of a cat?

5   *Coffee*
   i) Which substance makes coffee a stimulant?
   ii) Where did coffee originate?
   iii) What colour are the berries when ripe?
   iv) How is instant coffee made?

6   *Easter*
   i) What are Easter eggs the symbol of?
   ii) What does the word 'Easter' come from?

7   *Gladiator*
   i) What is meant by the word 'gladiator' and from which language is it derived?
   ii) When did gladiatorial combats begin in Rome?
   iii) Which types of person usually became gladiators?

8 *Newspapers*

    i) What was the first printed publication that came out at regular intervals in England?

    ii) What was the first daily paper in England and what was it called?

    iii) Under what name did *The Times* first appear, and in which year?

9 *Hundred Years War*

    i) Between which years did this war take place?

    ii) What was the name of the girl who led the French in raising the siege of Orleans in 1429?

    iii) What happened to her after this event?

    iv) What was left to the English in France at the end of the war?

10 *Mount Everest*

    i) In which mountain range and between which two countries is Mount Everest situated?

    ii) Who was it named after?

    iii) How many climbing expeditions had there been before the successful one in 1953?

    iv) Who are Sherpas?

5   To answer the following questions, you will need to refer to an encyclopedia. The key-words are printed in *italics*: look these words up in the encyclopedia you use as the starting-point for your search for the information you need. Thus in the first question, the word *Achilles* is printed in italics. Look up the entry for Achilles in the encyclopedia and see if the answer to the question about the Achilles tendon can be found there: if not, try another encyclopedia.

    i) What is an *Achilles* tendon? Why has it been given this name?

    ii) What is an *aurora*? How did it get its name?

    iii) When did *Braille* invent his system? Explain how it works.

    iv) What is a cantilever *bridge*?

    v) What do cumulo-nimbus *clouds* look like?

    vi) Describe what is known about the childhood of Charles *Dickens*.

vii) What does the word *eskimo* mean?
viii) What is *fresco* painting?
ix) What are the names of the main kinds of *insect*?
x) What could *leeches* be used for?
xi) How many kinds of *lightning* are there?
xii) What message did Samuel *Morse* send on the first telegraph line in the USA?
xiii) What are *numismatics*?
xiv) What is the *Pentathlon*?
xv) What is *porcelain*?

For the remaining questions, you will have to decide which is the keyword to look up:

xvi) Which is the largest rodent?
xvii) What is a seismograph?
xviii) In which African countries is Swahili spoken?
xiv) Hurricanes and typhoons are kinds of tropical storms: how are they different?
xx) Explain the difference between virus and bacteria.

4 Dictionaries: definition, abbreviation, derivation

Dictionaries are arranged alphabetically. They are useful in helping us to spell words correctly. They also provide *definitions* of the meanings of words, and explanations of their *derivations* (of how they came to be formed).

I   *Definition*: Stating precise nature of ... meaning of word.

Here are some words, and the dictionary definitions of their meanings. Unfortunately they are mixed up, so put the words into alphabetical order and then fit the definitions to the words they belong to:

hammer	—gnat, female of which punctures skin of man and animals with long proboscis and sucks their blood
island	—reptile (freq. huge) of mesozoic era
draught	—stout glove with long loose wrist for driving, fencing, wicket-keeping, etc.
tractor	—umbrella-shaped apparatus of silk, etc., allowing person or heavy object to descend safely from a height, esp. an aircraft

gauntlet	—neckband, upright or turned over, of coat, dress, shirt, etc.
dinosaur	—instrument for beating, breaking, driving nails, etc., with hard solid (usu. steel) head at right angles to handle
mosquito	—many-legged anthropod of class Chilopoda
parachute	—current of air in confined space (room, chimney, etc.)
collar	—self-propelled vehicle for hauling other vehicles, farm machinery, etc.
centipede	—piece of land surrounded by water

Only one of several possible definitions for 'draught' was given in the above list. How many other meanings for this word can you work out? Check with the definitions given in your dictionary.

2　Imagine you are compiling a dictionary. Make up your definitions for the following words—then check your explanations of their meanings with those given by the definitions of your dictionary (occasionally a word may have more than one meaning!):

　bat bicycle binoculars biscuit bonfire boomerang
　boutique bowl brake brush

3　*Abbreviate*: make short (usu. of writing part of word for whole)

　Thus *usu* in the above definition is an abbreviation of *usually*, just as *f* is an abbreviation of *from*, and *F* of French.

　What do the following abbreviations mean? You will often come across these abbreviations when using an encyclopedia or other reference book:

　anon.　c. or *circa*　cf　ed.　e.g.　ff.　i.e.　ibid.
　illus.　p. or pp.　q.v.　*vide*　viz.　vol.

4　*Derivation*: obtaining from a source; formation of word from word or root, tracing or statement of this (from French *derivation* or Latin *derivatio*).

　Many English words come from Latin, Greek and other languages. Some dictionaries tell you from which language an English word is derived, e.g.

　'castanets'—instruments of wood or ivory, attached to dancer's fingers to rattle in time with dancing. (From L *castanea*, chestnut.)

The derivation of 'dinosaur' given in the dictionary from which the definitions on page 16 have been quoted (the *Concise Oxford Dictionary*) is

> f. mod. L *dinosaurus* f. Gk, *deinos*, terrible + *sayrism* lizard

In the quiz on page 12 you were asked to find the derivations of 'Easter' and 'gladiator'. Here are the derivations of these words given in the *Concise Oxford Dictionary*:

> Easter—OE *ēastre*, pl. *ēastron*, OHG *ōstarūn* app. f. *Ēostre* goddess with festival in spring.
> gladiator—L *gladius*, sword.

Near the front of the *Concise Oxford Dictionary* there is a list of the abbreviations (shortenings) of words used in the dictionary. By looking up the abbreviations in this list, we find that

> f. mod. L = from modern Latin; f. Gk = from Greek and OE = Old English, pl. = plural, OHG = Old High German, and app. = apparently

a) Using the same abbreviations as those given in your dictionary, say from which language each of the following words is derived:

bandit	caravan	ranch
bazaar	garage	sofa
biscuit	jungle	tea
boomerang	loot	waltz
boutique	poodle	yacht

b) Which gods are these words named after? martial
morphia
volcano

c) The word 'bonfire' was originally 'bonefire'—why?
If your library has an etymological dictionary (one that explains the origins of words), it may give you more information than one of the other large dictionaries in the Reference section. Find out how these words began:

alibi	cardigan	lunatic
bedlam	good-bye	pasteurize
blancmange	gypsy	sandwich
bonfire	handicap	scapegoat
breakfast	journey	spinster

d)   'bicycle and 'binoculars' begin with the same two letters. Here are the derivations for these words:

F, f. *Bi–*, 2 + Gk *kuklos*, wheel
L *bini*, two together + *oculus*, eye

Look up the meanings of these words in a dictionary:

antechamber	anticyclone
antediluvian	antidote
antenatal	antimacassar
ante meridien	antipodes

Can you work out the difference in meaning between *ante–* and *anti–*?

5 The Title Page and Contents

1 *The Title Page*

a) Take any book from the non-fiction section of your library and turn to its *title page*. Use this page to answer the following questions:

—what is the full title of the book?
—what is the name of the author?
—what is the name of the publisher who published it? (Usually you will find this information at the bottom of the page.)

b) Turn the title page over (it is called the title page verso— why?), and find out:

—the date when the book was published (why is this information useful?);
—where the book was printed;
—whether the book has been reprinted, and if so how many times;
—whether the book has been revised—that is, brought up to date, or improved (for instance by adding more information). This is sometimes shown by the word *Edition*: '2nd Edition 1967, 3rd Edition 1975.'

c) What does © or the word Copyright mean? Look this word up in a dictionary. Why is it necessary to add this information to the date when the book was published?

d) This information about the book you have chosen comes at the front of the book. Is there any more information about the book you can find out before you read it?

e) Can you say—before reading through the book—what the book is about? How do you know?

2   *Contents*—summary of subject-matter of book, usually list of titles of chapters, etc. (*Concise Oxford Dictionary*)
Here are the titles of five books:

> *The Antarctic*
> *The Book of the Horse*
> *English Life in the Seventeenth Century*
> *Sea Fights Under Sail*
> *Stars and Space*

Listed below are the Contents of these books, but their titles are missing. Read through each list of chapters, then say which is the title of the book that you think contains them.
Can you fit each title to its list of Contents?

(*i*)

Contents			page
Chapter	1	Guns and Sails	7
Chapter	2	Lepanto	15
Chapter	3	The Spanish Armada	25
Chapter	4	The Four Days's Battle	37
Chapter	5	Barfleur and the French Corsairs	47
Chapter	6	Quiberon Bay	55
Chapter	7	American Independence	65
Chapter	8	St Vincent and Camperdown	77
Chapter	9	The Nile and Trafalgar	87
Chapter	10	Anglo-American Duels	105
Chapter	11	Navarino	117

(*ii*)

Contents			page
Chapter	1	The Universe Around Us	4
Chapter	2	Our home, the Earth	7
Chapter	3	Looking Into Space	10
Chapter	4	Travel to other Worlds	14
Chapter	5	Our Companion, the Moon	18
Chapter	6	The Glory of the Sun	22

(*iii*)

Contents

(*iv*)

Contents

(*v*)

Contents

3   Now give the title of the book, and the number of the chapter in which you could find out more about the following topics from the contents lists above:

> (*Example*: The battle of Lepanto—*Sea Fights Under Sail*, Chapter 2.)

   i) Seals
  ii) The Fire of London, 1666
 iii) What happened at the Battle of Trafalgar
 iv) *a)* Life on Mars   *b)* Life on Venus
  v) Pegasus, the winged horse of Greek mythology
 vi) Penguins
vii) The Spanish attempt to invade Britain in 1588
viii) Space travel
 ix) How to look after a pony
  x) Telescopes

Whereabouts in a book will you find its list of Contents?

4   '*Contents*—summary of subject-matter of book ...'
Just by looking through the list of Contents of a book, you can work out very quickly what the book is likely to be about—its *subject-matter*. For instance, from reading the Contents of *The Antarctic*, we find that this book tells us about the physical conditions of the region (ice, weather, etc.), the animals that live there, and how man has explored this part of the world and settled there.

Read through the Contents of *The Book of the Horse* and *Stars and Space* again, and say briefly what you think is the subject-matter of these books.

5   Now find a book in the non-fiction section of your library on one of the following topics:

Africa	food
ancient history	music
animals	the Second World War
buildings	sport
clothes	transport

Make brief notes under these headings:

> *Title*
> *Author*
> *Subject-matter*

6 The Contents of *The Antarctic* also includes

List of Colour Illustrations	i
Preface	ix
Acknowledgements	x

a) What is a *Preface* (sometimes this is called a *Foreword*)? If you don't know, see if you can find a non-fiction book that has one, and work out what this term means by finding out what the preface to the book you choose tells you.

b) What does the term *Acknowledgements* mean?

c) The page references for the Preface and Acknowledgements are given in roman numerals—can you suggest why?

d) At the end of the list of Contents for *The Antarctic*, there is

Appendix A—Further Reading	252
Appendix B—Antarctic Treaty, 1959	256
Appendix C—The Organization of Antarctic Research	262
Appendix D—Stations Operating in the Antarctic	267
Index	269

What do the terms *Appendix* and *Index* mean? (If you are not sure, look ahead to pages 78–82, and the next chapter of this book.)

6   The Index

1   You found the subject-matter of the book by reading through its Contents, which appears at or near the beginning of the book. Whereabouts would you look to find the Index?

What is the difference between the Contents and the Index of a book?

You use the Contents to find out a book's subject matter. What do you use an Index for?

Here is the Index of one of the books whose Contents you have read through already (*Stars and Space*) on page 20.

Index

As you can see, the Index, like the Contents, is also a list, but the items in the Index are listed in a different way. Can you explain the difference?

2   The numbers refer to pages in the book. So you will find out about Albireo on page 44, and Dwarf stars on page 46. Occasionally, there may be two, or even several pages dealing with a topic:

> Saturn, 5, 32–33
> stars 38–48
> telescopes 10–13

Find the entries for 'stars' and 'telescopes' in the Index printed above. You will see that there are more references to these items, but they are concerned with more specific aspects of the topic:

> telescopes 10–13
>   home-made, 11, 12
>   radio, 50, 54

The first reference is concerned with telescopes generally—on pages 10, 11, 12, and 13. If you want to find out about home-made telescopes, there is no need to read through pages 10 and 13—and you won't find anything about radio telescopes on any of these pages, but need to turn to another part of the book, pages 50 and 54.

If you look back at the Contents list on page 20 and at your answer to (x) on page 22 you will notice that pages 10–13 appear in Chapter 3—indeed (as your answer probably indicated) the whole of this chapter is about telescopes. But pages 50 and 54, where you will find reference to radio telescopes, are in another chapter—which? Did your answer to (x) include this chapter?

This example helps to explain the difference between the Contents and the Index of a book. By looking at the Contents you can form an idea of the general subject-matter of the book, and perhaps of each chapter: but to find out information about particular details, you need to consult the Index.

So you can find out the information a non-fiction book can give you in more than one way.

First, of course, there is the *title*: *Stars and Space* which tells you that the book is about aspects of astronomy, but doesn't make it clear whether these aspects include, for instance, space travel. Perhaps the publisher tells you more about the book in the *blurb* on the cover:

'Patrick Moore gives the latest information about what has been, and can be seen in the night sky; about space exploration; about the composition of the Moon and planets; about galaxies and quasars. Actual photographs replace many of the diagrams in previous editions.'

Does the information in the blurb tell you anything that you hadn't already worked out by reading through the Contents?

The 'actual photographs' will also give you an indication of the subject-matter of the book. These, together with the title, the Contents and (if there is one) the blurb will tell you if the book is likely to contain information about the topic you want to find out about, and would be perfectly sufficient if you wanted to read the whole book, or certain chapters of the book, out of a general interest in the book's subject-matter. But if you want to find a book that will tell you about telescopes, then you need to look quickly through the books on the shelves in the astronomy section of your library, and find out if any of them can help you. As we have seen, the Contents has shown that there is a chapter that is likely to be useful. The Index, though, at the back of the book, is more useful still—particularly if you want to find out about a particular item, such as radio telescopes. By looking up the pages referred to in the Index, you can see quickly whether there is the information about radio telescopes that you need—without having to read through the whole of the book first. Perhaps additional information, or more detailed information on this topic is to be found in another book by Patrick Moore in the library (or by another author): if so, the Index in that book will help you to find out where the information you need is.

3   Now, referring to the Index to *Stars and Space*, say which pages you would refer to if you wanted to find out about

    i) stars generally
    ii) the sizes of stars
    iii) Moon craters
    iv) the Southern Cross
    v) shooting-stars
    vi) comets
    vii) the Milky Way
    viii) the Plough
    ix) planets generally (which pages would you read first?)
    x) eclipses of the Sun.

4   Choose three of the topics listed above, and find out which books in the astronomy section of your library give the most detailed information about them.

7 Classification of non-fiction books and the Dewey Decimal System

When using the non-fiction section of the library for reserch, remember to put the subject you are looking for under a general heading before trying to find the books that will give you information about it. Like the librarian, you have to *classify*.

1 How are the books in the *Non-Fiction* section of your library arranged?

Add the following labels to your plan (see page 2) to show where books on these topics can be found:

   biography   travel   sport   history   science   religion

2 What is the Dewey System? Why is it called the Dewey *Decimal* System? To answer these questions, look at the spines of any of the books in the Non-Fiction section of your library: can you find their Dewey numbers? Where can you see this number apart from on the spine of a book? What does this number tell you?

3 The Dewey number is another pointer to the subject-matter of the non-fiction books in your library, helping you to find books on topics that interest you. Just as the manager of a supermarket tries to arrange the goods for sale in a sensible order so that his customers can easily find what they want to buy, so the books in a library are placed on the shelves for readers to be able to locate them easily. The books are *classified*: that is, they are arranged in groups or classes. We have seen how stories in the Fiction section of the library are arranged alphabetically (pages 6–9), and so are entries in dictionaries and encyclopedias in the General Reference section (pages 10, 15). The stories are arranged alphabetically according to their authors (books written by someone called *Brown* would come before those written by an author whose name is *Green*), and the encyclopedias are arranged alphabetically according to their subject entries (*Coal* comes before *Iron*). Books in the Non-Fiction section of the library are arranged according to their subjects, too, but not in alphabetical order.

Most libraries use the Dewey System to classify their non-fiction books. Melvin Dewey, an American, divided all knowledge into ten parts. His system of classification uses numbers for its code and it is called the Dewey *Decimal* System. Thus the 'code number' for birds is 598.2 and all the books about birds in one library will be found together with this classification number. Similarly, the Dewey number for astronomy is 520, so Patrick Moore's book *Stars and Planets* will be found with the other books that have 520 on their spines.

Which Dewey numbers fit the labels you have added to the Non-Fiction section in your plan of your library? Find out by checking the numbers on the spines of the books on the biography, travel, sport, history and religion shelves.

The ten main classes are as follows:

000	General	—reference books (e.g. *The Guinness Book of Records, The Oxford Junior Encyclopedia*)
100	Philosophy	
200	Religion	
300	Social Sciences	—including books about how the country is organized, e.g. government, defence, trade, laws, education (including careers), customs, etc. You will thus find books on stamps in this section—classified under the heading Postal Communications 383.2
400	Languages	
500	Science	

600 Useful Arts (sometimes called Applied Science, or Technology) —including medicine, transport, agriculture (so you will find books on animal husbandry here—including the care of pets), cooking, and manufacturing industries

700 Fine Arts —including music, drama, painting, sport, hobbies

800 Literature —including plays, poems, books about writers (but stories are usually arranged separately in the fiction section of the library)

900 Geography, Biography and History —books on places, people and events. Books in the Biography section 920 are, like fiction, arranged alphabetically—according to the name of the person whose life is written about.

Each of the ten main classes is divided into ten divisions, making a total of one hundred divisions. There is no point in trying to remember them all. To start with, learn the ten main divisions and try to place the subject you want to read about in one of the ten main classes. So, if you want to find out about how a house is built you need to think of the 'Useful Arts' main class—building—but if you are doing a project on church architecture (for instance, wanting to find out about the artistic styles of cathedrals in the 12th—15th centuries), then you need to look in the Fine Arts class. Geography often causes a problem: to begin with, remember that books on physical geography (books about rocks, for instance, or weather) are classified under 550, while books about countries are classified under 910 onwards.

Some of the hundred divisions are worth remembering now, as they are popular subjects:

510 Mathematics
520 Astronomy
550 Physical Geography (e.g. rocks and weather)
560 Paleontology (fossils, dinosaurs, etc)
580 Botany (plants, trees)
590 Zoology (animals)
620 Engineering (including TV, transport—i.e. how cars, ships, trains, planes are made)
720 Architecture
780 Music

790 Sport, Hobbies
910 Ancient History, Archaeology
920 Biography
940 European History
970 North American History

4   Here are two lists—one of Dewey numbers in numerical order, and the other of subjects in alphabetical order. Write out the list of Dewey numbers, and add to each number the subject it is concerned with, e.g.

Dewey Number			*Subject*
520			*Astronomy*

200	600	720	910
440	610	730	920
510	620	740	930
520	630	750	940
540	640	760	950
550		770	960
560		780	970
570		790	980
580			
590			

African history
agriculture
ancient history
anthropology (study of
    mankind, esp. of races,
    customs, evolution)
architecture
Asian history
astronomy
biography
botany (study of plants)
chemistry
drawing
earth sciences (e.g. geology)
engineering
European history
French language
geography, travel
home economics, homecraft
mathematics
medicine
music
North American history
painting
paleontology (life in geological
    past, e.g. fossils, dinosaurs)
photography
prints and printmaking
recreations and hobbies
religion
science
sculpture
South American history
technology
zoology (study of animals)

The third digit in all of these Dewey numbers is 0, which shows that books classified (grouped) under these numbers deal with the subjects generally. So 600, for example, is about technology generally, and 620 refers to an aspect of technology, engineering generally. A more detailed classification can be given by changing the third digit. Find out which engineering subjects are dealt with by books classified according to these Dewey numbers:

621	624	627
622	625	628
623	626	629

You have probably noticed that some of the Dewey numbers on non-fiction books have decimal points, e.g. 629.1 These help the Librarian to classify books in a more detailed order. So 940 refers to the general history of Europe, and

940.1 refers to Medieval Europe (that is, the years 476–1453 AD)

940.2 to the years 1453–1914

940.3 to the causes of the First World War

940.4 to the military history of the First World War

940.5 to 20th-Century Europe

940.53 deals with the Second World War, and 940.54 refers to its military history, while 940.55 concerns Europe since the Second World War.

5   By looking at the Dewey numbers on the books on the shelves of the non-fiction section of the library, make a list of the subjects dealt with by books classified 590–599 and 790–799:

590	790
591	791
592	792
593	793
594	794
595	795
597	796
597	797
598	798
599	799

6   When looking for a book on the non-fiction shelves, think first of a general heading—e.g. *sport* for a book on improving your technique as a goalkeeper—and think of another way to describe your topic—e.g. *association football*, or *soccer* for football (as distinguished from rugby football, for instance).

Give general headings for these topics that would help you to find books about them in the non-fiction section of your library:

i) dinosaurs	xii) hawks
ii) the life of Napoleon	xiii) sea fishing
iii) Mars	xiv) growing vegetables
iv) the voyages of Captain Cook	xv) the sculpture of Barbara Hepworth
v) how to bake a cake	xvi) how an electric light bulb works
vi) keeping gerbils or hamsters	xvii) the river Amazon
vii) pottery	xviii) the Spanish Armada, 1588
viii) volleyball	
ix) car maintenance	xix) the discovery of penicillin
x) red Indians	
xi) the Aztecs	xx) elephants

7   Sometimes the topic you want to find out about may be dealt with by books in more than one subject area of the library. For instance, if you wanted to find out about the eruptions of Vesuvius, you would would need to look in the shelves where you will find books about volcanoes (550 Earth Sciences) and also books on the history of Pompeii (913 Archeology); you might also find information in the travel section (914), in a guide to southern Italy, for instance.

In which subject areas of the non-fiction section of your library would you look for books on the following topics? (e.g. Queen Elizabeth I—942 English History, and 920 Biography).

i) Railways in Victorian England
ii) Nelson, H.M.S. *Victory* and the Battle of Trafalgar
iii) South American snakes
iv) Costume designs for a historical play by Shakespeare
v) Roman roads
vi) Ancient Greek myths
vii) Mount Everest
viii) Famous cathedrals in France
ix) Buffaloes
x) Buster Keaton, Charles Chaplin, and other stars of the silent movies

8 The Catalogue and Library Quiz

Catalogue—complete list, usu. alphabetical or under headings.

A Library Catalogue is the complete list of all books in that particular library. In your School Library the catalogue is probably a cabinet with drawers containing cards on which there is information about the books. In other libraries the catalogue may take a different form; for instance, the books may be catalogued on microfilm or in book form.

1 Often the information stored in the cards which make up the library catalogue can be useful to you, because frequently you find that the books you need are out on loan. So if, for example, after looking at the books on the shelves, you cannot find stories by the author whose books you have previously enjoyed, or you cannot find books dealing with a topic about which you want to find information, use the catalogue to find out whether the library has the books that you are looking for.

Can you think of other occasions when the catalogue might be useful?

a) Here is a catalogue card:

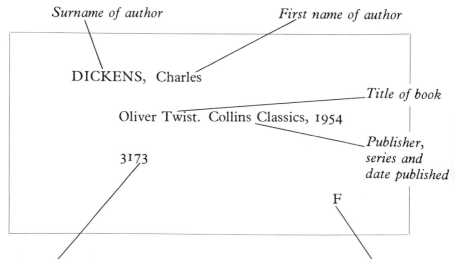

Surname of author   *First name of author*

DICKENS, Charles

Title of book

Oliver Twist. Collins Classics, 1954

Publisher,
series and
date published

3173

F

Accession number—i.e. this was
the three thousand one hundred and
seventy-third book to be bought for
the library

In some library catalogues there is
also the letter F—to show
that this book is a story in
the Fiction section of the
library

Here is another catalogue card:

999   KING, H. G. R.

The Antarctic. Blandford Press, 1969

15702

b)   i) Which number is the Dewey number?
   ii) In which section of the library would you look to find this
       book?
  iii) Where would you look in the catalogue if you wanted to
       read other books by H. G. R. King?

```
Lorna Doone

BLACKMORE, R. D.

English Literature Series, 1935

476
                                    F
```

c)   i) What kind of catalogue card is the one shown above?
    ii) Is this book fiction or non-fiction?
    iii) How do you know that this book was not written by Lorna
        Doone?
    iv) How do you know that this book was not bought by the
        library recently?
d)   i) What cards are likely to be on either side of this card for
        Patrick Moore's book, *Stars and Space*?

```
520   MOORE, Patrick

        Stars and Space. A&C Black, 1972

        16907
```

    ii) How can this card help you to find this book on your
        library shelves?
    iii) What does 'A&C Black, 1972' mean?

2   (*For individual/small group work*)
a)   Draw a plan of the drawers of the catalogue cabinet. Label each
     drawer (e.g. Subject Index, Fiction Authors, etc.).
        Underneath your drawing of the catalogue cabinet make a
     list of the labels and explain what they mean.

b) Choose one non-fiction book and one novel on the shelves of your library. Make a note of their titles, authors and publishers (this information should be on the spine of the books—if not, look at the title page) and, in the case of the non-fiction book, its Dewey number. Using this information, find the books' cards in the catalogue. Copy the cards and add the following labels to your drawings of them:

author title publisher accession number classification (i.e. F—for the novel, Dewey Number for the non-fiction book.)

Add to your drawings a note explaining what each of these terms means.

c) Think of a subject that interests you; then using the catalogue choose three books that are concerned with this subject. See if the books are on the library shelves: if they are, look at their lists of contents, illustrations, etc., and say which book interests you most, and why.

3 In which drawers of the catalogue would you find cards that would give you the following information?

i) you have read a book about cinephotography and wonder whether there are any other books on this subject out on loan (you have already checked the library shelves but can only find two books, both of which you don't want as they are written for beginners);

ii) you have read two stories by a novelist that you have enjoyed very much and know she has written several more but you can't find any on the shelves;

iii) you want to do a project on the history of transport and want to find out what is available;

iv) recently you borrowed a book about snakes and you want to borrow it again, but you can't find it on the shelves and the Librarian can't reserve it for you without knowing the author;

v) you have been given a book token as a birthday present and think you would like to use it to buy a book you have enjoyed reading from the library: the bookseller will order the book for you if you can name the book's publisher.

4-6 This chapter ends with a quiz. To answer it you will need to refer to encyclopedias or books in the non-fiction section of the library. Before trying this quiz look through the first group of statements about animals in **4.** You have to say whether these statements are true or false.

Before you can find the book that will help you, you must know what you are looking for:

—If you try an encyclopedia you will have to think of the key word in the statement (see page 13)—in i) it will be *bat*, in ii) *beaver*, and so on. However, if you find that the entry under *bat* in your encyclopedia doesn't tell you about any species of bat that catches fish, this doesn't necessarily mean that the statement in i) is false. You will have to look at other books in the non-fiction section of the library to make sure.

—The non-fiction section is much bigger than the general reference section so you must first of all put the statements in this quiz under a general heading. Obviously, after looking through them all, you can see that all the statements in **4** are about animals, so you then need to find where the books on animals are kept— and if you know the Dewey number (see pages 78–81), this can help you find them more easily.

—When you get to the books on animals, again think of general headings: for instance, there may not be any books about beavers, but if you think of the type of animal the beaver is, or where it is found in the wild, that may help you.

—When you have decided on the books that may be useful, then use the *Index* to help you find the pages where the information you need may be found (see pages 24–27).

4   Some of these statements are true and some are false.

   i) A species of bat catches fish.
  ii) A beaver can hold its breath for as long as 15 minutes and swim for half a mile under water.
 iii) Lions are scavengers—they steal prey from other animals.
  iv) Only male mosquitoes bite humans.
   v) The barn owl is found in every continent except the Antarctic.
 vii) The duck-billed platypus is the only mammal that lays eggs.
viii) A tiger is larger than a lion.

Check these statements by referring to books in the non-fiction section of the Library (look for the Dewey numbers 590–599) and encyclopedias. When you have found out whether a statement is true or false, explain how you did so by:

   i) giving the title of the book that gives the answer, and
  ii) quoting the words in the book that prove that the statement is true or false.

5   What is the Dewey number for books about Astronomy? (see page 79). You will need to find this out before checking the next group of statements.

 i) There are seasons on Mars.
 ii) Mars is the nearest planet to the Sun.
 iii) Mars is further from the Sun than it is from Earth.
 ii) The Moon is half the size of the Earth.
 v) Pluto goes round the Sun once every 247 years.
 vi) The Sun doesn't move.
viii) The temperature on Venus is 400 degrees hotter than that of the Earth at its surface.

When you say whether a statement is true or false make sure you justify your answer by giving your source of information—the title of the book—and quoting the evidence it gives, in the same way as you did when checking the statements in 4 above.

6   The final group of statements are not confined to one subject area: so you will have to decide which shelves in the non-fiction section of the library are most likely to have books where you can find out which of these statements are true and which are false.

 i) The Amazon is the longest river in the world.
 ii) The weather in the Arctic is much colder than that in the Antarctic.
 iii) The USA is larger than Australia.
 iv) Leonardo da Vinci invented the parachute.
 v) Henry VIII had seven wives, all of whom were executed.
 vi) Dandelion, deadly nightshade, foxgloves, holly, laburnum, mistletoe and rhubarb leaves are all poisonous.
 vii) The battle of Trafalgar was fought on a Monday.
viii) The oldest cathedral in the British Isles is Canterbury.
 ix) The first passenger train service came into operation in 1836.
 x) The potato was introduced to Europe by Sir Francis Drake.

Section Two: Library Assignments

Introduction

Before you try any of the assignments in this section, read the following notes very carefully:

When using books:

1   Glance through them, noting the

Title: Does it seem to be about what you are studying?
Author: Have you read any books by him before, and if so, were they helpful?
Date of Publication: Is the book up-to-date?
Blurb: You will find this on the cover, or in the front of the book. Does it tell you what the book is about, and if so, does it seem useful?
Introduction
Contents page: Choose those chapter headings which seem useful for your topic
Index: Make a note of the pages in the book which seem to have information on the particular points for which you are looking

Remember (i) that many books contain useful information which is not always suggested by the title of the book. Both the contents page and the index will help you. (See pages 19–27);

    (ii) Some non-fiction books also have a separate contents page for maps/diagrams/photographs, all of which can be very helpful.

2   Skim (read quickly) through the chapters and pages you have chosen. As you do so, you may be able to think of more questions about your topic to which you would like to find the answers. The clearer you are about what you are looking for, the more likely you are to succeed. Write the questions down in your note book.

The first and last paragraphs of each chapter and the first and last sentences of each paragraph can be helpful to you. The first paragraph usually tells you what the chapter is about, and the last one often summarizes what has been said. Similarly the first and last sentences of a paragraph will sometimes give you an idea of its contents. This will help you to decide whether it is worth reading the whole chapter or paragraph.

During this preparatory work, you should make a note of which pages in the book you need to read again more thoroughly. It is not often necessary to read a whole book all the way through. You can then set about reading the portions chosen.

3   It is important to make some rough notes about what you have read, before going on to write up, or talk about, the information you have gained. It is a waste of time to copy large portions of a book out. It usually means that you have not understood it and will not remember it. It is better to read a section or chapter through, and then note briefly the main points that you learned from it. When you have finished you can glance back to check that you have noted them correctly. If you do this with all that you read for information (obviously this does not include books that you read only for pleasure), you can then compare notes made from the various books, pamphlets etc. that you have chosen, and if you find that they disagree, you can check the information again somewhere else. *Always keep a note of the title and author of any books you have used.*

9 Look it up!

How many of these questions can you answer correctly? Use encyclopedias and books in the non-fiction section of your library to help you find the information you need; and make a note of the title of the book (and the number of the page) where you get the information from—in case you need to prove it!

I   a)   Where is

      i) the Eiffel Tower?
      ii) the White House?
      iii) the Taj Mahal?
      iv) the Acropolis?
      v) the Bridge of Sighs?

    b)   What is the name of the capital city of

      i) Argentina?
      ii) Brazil?
      iii) Bulgaria?
      iv) Canada?
      v) Egypt?
      vi) Holland?

    vii) India?

   viii) Japan?

    ix) Thailand?

     x) Yugoslavia?

c) Draw and colour the flags of the member countries of the Common Market.

2 a) How far is it by road from London to the following cities?

i) Aberdeen	vi) Glasgow
ii) Birmingham	vii) Leeds
iii) Bristol	viii) Liverpool
iv) Cardiff	ix) Newcastle
v) Exeter	x) Southampton

b) Which cities can you travel to by train from these main-line termini in London? Give the names of 3 cities for each station.

i) Euston	ii) King's Cross	iii) Paddington
iv) Victoria	v) Waterloo	

c) What is the time in the following cities when it is noon in London? Find a World Time Chart to help you work out how many hours you need to add or subtract from the time in this country.

i) Buenos Aires	vi) New York
ii) Cairo	vii) Peking
iii) Delhi	viii) Rome
iv) Mexico	ix) San Francisco
v) Nairobi	x) Tokyo

3 a) Copy pictures of two different kinds of

    i) hunting dog;

   ii) the fish found in the Pacific Ocean;

   iii) wildflowers you might find growing in a wood in spring.

b) Make drawings to illustrate the life cycle of either a butterfly or a frog.

c) Draw the leaves of i) an ash tree; ii) an oak tree; iii) a sycamore tree.

4 a) Draw a diagram of one of the following types of building and label the chief parts:

i) a Roman villa; ii) a medieval castle; iii) a cathedral.

b) Make drawings to illustrate what the windows of houses would look like in i) Elizabethan England (the late 16th century); and ii) Georgian England (the 18th century).

c) Make drawings to illustrate the clothes worn by people who would have lived in the houses you have drawn in b).

5 Here are two lists—one of discoveries and inventions, and another of the names and dates of the people who made them. Rearrange the lists so that the names of the people match the names of their discoveries.

i) antiseptic surgery
   aspirin
   cyanide
   oxygen
   penicillin
   radioactivity
   radium
   uranium fission
      (atomic reactor)

Fermi and Szilard 1942
Fleming 1929
Dreser 1889
Curie 1896
Caro 1905
Priestley 1774
Lister 1867
Becquerel 1896

ii) adding machine
    air conditioning
    barometer
    bicycle
    cash register
    cement
    dynamite
    electric lamp

Edison 1879
Nobel 1867
Ritty 1879
Vicat 1824
Macmillan 1839
Torricelli 1643
Pascal 1642
Carrier 1911

iii) gramophone
     hovercraft
     jet engine
     lightning conductor
     margarine
     match (safety)
     microscope
     nylon
     piano

Carothers 1937
Edison 1878
Cristofori 1729
Whittle 1929
Cockerell 1955
Janssen 1590
Franklin 1752
Mege-Mouries 1863
Lundstrom 1855
Judson 1891

iv) radio
    radar

    safety pin

Shockley, Brittain and Bardeen 1947
Galileo 1593

safety razor	Marconi 1896
telephone	Burt 1829
thermometer	Watson-Watt 1935
transistor	Hunt 1849
typewriter	Henson 1847
zip fastener	Reis 1861, Bell 1876

6   a)   Which country won the World Cup in i) 1974; ii) 1970; iii) 1966?

      b)   Which player holds the record for the greatest number of goals scored in a career? How many goals did he score?

      c)   What is the world's highest reported transfer fee for a footballer? Name the player, the club that paid the fee, and the amount paid.

7   a)   Give the world records for the following athletic events, together with the names of the athletes who hold them (give the records for both men and women if they are available):

         i) 100 metres; ii) 3000 metres; iii) high jump; iv) long jump; v) shot; vi) discus; vii) javelin.

      b)   In which countries have the last three Olympic Games and Winter Olympics been held?

      c)   Who holds the world record for the following swimming events (give the name and the time for both men and women record holders):

         i) freestyle; ii) backstroke; iii) breaststroke; iv) butterfly.

8   a)   How many test matches have been won by i) England; ii) Australia; iii) West Indies; iv) India; v) Pakistan? Which country has won the highest proportion of matches played?

      b)   Which bowler holds the record for the most wickets in a test series?

      c)   Which batsman holds the record for the highest number of runs scored in one day?

9   a)   What do these musical terms mean?

         i) adagio; ii) allegro; iii) andante; iv) crescendo; v) diminuendo; vi) dolce; vii) forte; viii) largo; ix) pianissimo; x) presto.

b)   When did these painters live, and what were their nationalities? (e.g. Franz Hals—? 1580–1666, Dutch)

i) John Constable; ii) William Hogarth; iii) Pablo Picasso; iv) Michelangelo; v) Rembrandt; vi) Renoir; vii) El Greco; viii) Vincent van Gogh; ix) Leonardo da Vinci.

c)   Find out when these composers lived and arrange them in chronological order, i.e., the one who lived the longest ago first:

i) J. S. Bach; ii) Beethoven; iii) Britten; iv) Chopin v) Dvorak; vi) Handel; vii) Holst; viii) Mozart; ix) Tchaikovsky; x) Wagner.

10   a)   Give the name of one book and its date of publication for each of the following writers:

Jane Austen	Charles Dickens	Charlotte Bronte
Emily Bronte	George Eliot	Thomas Hardy
H. G. Wells		

b)   Sort out these lists of poets and poems so that each poem matches the poet who wrote it:

Geoffrey Chaucer	Paradise Lost
Robert Burns	Canterbury Tales
John Keats	Goblin Market
Edward Lear	Ode to Autumn
John Milton	The Owl and the Pussycat
Christina Rossetti	Tam O'Shanter

c)   Here is a list of famous writers. Find out when they lived and arrange them in chronological order, i.e. the one who lived longest ago first:

i) Louisa M. Alcott; ii) John Bunyan; iii) Agatha Christie; iv) Daniel Defoe; v) Ian Fleming; vi) Samuel Pepys; vii) Robert Louis Stevenson; viii) William Makepeace Thackeray; ix) Mark Twain; x) John Wyndham

11   Give the dates of the presidency or reign of each of the United States Presidents and English Kings and Queens in the following list:

i) George Washington
ii) Henry VIII
iii) Theodore Roosevelt

iv) Victoria
v) Abraham Lincoln
vi) Charles I
vii) Elizabeth I
viii) Franklin D. Roosevelt
ix) Edward the Confessor
x) Dwight D. Eisenhower
xi) James I
xii) Harry S. Truman
xiii) William and Mary
xiv) John F. Kennedy
xv) Richard I

12 i) Robert Baden-Powell, the founder of the Scouts movement, became famous for something he did in South Africa: what? What nickname did the Matabele tribe call him by?
ii) Why is Christopher Carson an American hero?
iii) What did these men have in common: Chippendale, Hepplewhite, Sheraton?
iv) Complete this sentence spoken by Sir Winston Churchill in 1940 when he became Prime Minister: 'I have nothing to offer but ...'
v) Two Americans called Cody, both alive in the second half of the nineteenth century, became famous for different reasons. What did Samuel Franklin Cody (1862–1913) and William Frederick Cody (1846–1917) do to become famous?
vi) The Pope forbade Christians to read a book by Nicolas Copernicus called *Concerning the Revolutions of the Heavenly Spheres*: why?
vii) In the English Civil War, Cromwell formed a regiment noted for its discipline: what was it called?
viii) In the American Civil War the cavalry officer Lieutenant George Armstrong Custer was called a different name by the Sioux: what? What was his 'last stand'?
ix) Several stories by Charles Dickens have scenes taking place in prison: what event in his childhood might have been in his mind when writing these scenes?
xi) What is the connection between Elizabeth Fry and the last question?

13 i) What were the seven wonders of the Ancient World?

   ii) Where is the hottest place on Earth, and where is the coldest?

  iii) What does a barometer do? How does it work?

  iv) Who discovered Australia?

   v) How many States are there in the U.S.A.?

  vi) Who made the first bicycle?

 vii) When was the first telephone message made, and who made it?

viii) Who built the first petrol-driven car? What was its top speed?

  ix) Who made the first flight by aeroplane across the English Channel, and on what date?

   x) In the 19th Century policemen were called Peelers—why?

14   i) Why do bees swarm?

   ii) Why don't polar bears slip and fall on the ice?

  iii) Why is the distance between the ears of an owl greater than in other birds?

  iv) How much does a fully grown hippopotamus weigh? What does its name mean?

   v) How does an octopus swim?

  vi) How many bones are there in a human skeleton?

 vii) How fast can a racehorse run?

viii) How do insects breathe?

  ix) Besides not being able to fly, how does an ostrich differ from other birds?

   x) What should you do if you are bitten by a snake?

10 Topics for research

A. Animals

1 In which parts of the world do the following animals live in the wild?

> antelopes camels chimpanzees elephants giraffes
> gorillas hippopotamuses kangaroos llamas orang-utans

2 Draw a horse and label the following parts of its body:

> forelock poll mane withers muzzle coronet
> forearm fetlock elbow pastern gaskin hock

3   a) What is the largest species of insect in this country?
b) What is the largest butterfly in this country?
c) How many species of spider are there in this country?
d) What is the most venomous spider in the world?
e) What is the largest spider in the world?
f) What is the smallest spider in this country?

4   To which animals do these tracks belong?

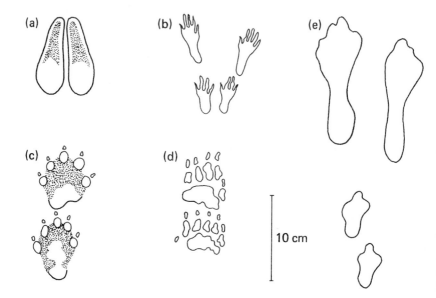

5   *Bees*
   a) Why do bees make honey? How is it formed? Describe
   what you would see if you looked inside a hive, and the
   work done by the worker bees there.
   c) How many eggs can a queen bee lay in a day?

6   *Bats*
   a) How do bats differ from birds?
   b) i) Are they blind?
      ii) What has man learned from bats in developing radar
      and sonar devices?
   c) What do bats eat?
   d) Find out as much as you can about vampire bats. Why
   are they dangerous?

7   *Coral*
   a) What is coral? How is it formed?
   b) Describe how coral islands and lagoons are formed.
   c) i) What is the Great Barrier Reef?
      ii) Which animal is threatening it? How can it be saved?

8   *Prehistoric Animals*
   Find out about any three of the following creatures, then give

brief details of what is known about each of them together with a sketch of what they looked like:

i) coelocanth; ii) diplodocus; iii) iguanodon; iv) pteranodon; v) meganeura; vi) tyrannosaurus.

9   *Extinct Animals*
Find out about any two of the following animals that are now extinct. Make a sketch of each animal you choose, then give brief notes of where it lived, and how it became extinct.

i) dodo; ii) great auk; iii) mammoth; iv) passenger pigeon; v) sabre-tooth tiger.

10   *Dogs*
a) How many different breeds of dog are there?
b) Which wild animals are related to the domestic dog?
c) i) Find out about how the dog developed from its ancestor Miacin.
    ii) When did this creature live?
d) i) How do dogs differ from wolves?
    ii) Find out about wolves, coyotes, jackals and dingos.
e) i) Describe as many examples as you can find of how dogs
are used by man to help him in his work.
    ii) Why is dog called man's best friend?

11   *Cats*
a)   Find out about the ancestor of the cat, Dinicitis, when
it lived, and how it was like modern cats
b)   i) Cats are *carnivores*: what does this mean?
     ii) Why won't a cat eat if it has a cold?
     iii) Why can cats see well in the dark?
c)   i) How do lions hunt and kill their prey?
     ii) Can they be beaten in a fight?
d)   Where do lions, tigers and leopards live in the wild?
e)   i) How does a jaguar differ from a leopard?
     ii) How does a cheetah differ from other big cats?
     iii) What other kinds of wild cat are there?

12   *Gorillas*
a) Gorillas, like gibbons and orang-utans, are apes—how
do gorillas differ from gibbons and orang-utans?
b) i) Gorillas travel in 'troops'—how many gorillas are there
in a troop?
    ii) How do they spend the day, and night?

      iii) What do they eat?
- c) i) How big is a fully-grown gorilla?
  - ii) How does it scare away its enemies?
- d) How old is a baby gorilla before it can walk and feed itself?
- e) Where do gorillas live in the wild?

13   *Spiders*
- a) How many types of spider are there in the world?
- b) i) How thick is a strand of a spider's silk?
  - ii) How is it made?
  - iii) How does a spider make its web?
- c) i) How does a spider catch and kill its prey?
  - ii) Do all spiders use the same method?
- d) i) Can tarantulas kill man?
  - ii) Large hairy tarantulas in America are often called bird-eating spiders. How big are they, and why are they called by this name?
- e) i) How many eyes does a spider have?
  - iii) How does it breathe?
- f) Why isn't a spider an insect?

14   *Dolphins*
- a) i) Dolphins have highly developed voices and hearing—why?
  - ii) How do they make use of them?
  - iii) Do they have good sight?
- b) Describe their habits.
  - i) Do they travel singly? Where, and how do they sleep?
  - ii) How do they feed?
  - iii) How does a mother feed her baby?
- c) i) How long can an active dolphin stay submerged?
  - ii) How are dolphins able to do this?
  - iii) How deep can they dive?
- d) i) How fast can a dolphin swim?
  - ii) How do dolphins propel themselves?
  - iii) How do they keep warm, and how do they keep cool?
- e) Dolphins are known to be very intelligent. Can you find any examples of this?

15   *Ants*
- a) Ants live in colonies. How many ants live in a typical colony?
- b) Describe a typical society of ants, the functions they

perform—the queen, the soldier ants, the workers, the doorkeeper.

c) Describe also

   i) how the eggs grow into larvae and pupae, and what happens

   ii) when ants swarm, and

   iii) when a queen grows old.

d) How do ants feed?

e) There are several ways in which ants build nests—describe some.

f) Some ants keep 'herds of cattle'

   i) What are they?

   ii) How do the ants look after them?

g) Find out as much as you can about the gardening ant, Atta the leaf-cutter.

16 *Butterflies*

a) The scientific name for butterflies, Lepidoptera, comes from the Latin word meaning 'scaly wings'—why should they be given this name?

b) How many different kinds of moths and butterflies exist in this country?

c) Explain the main differences between a moth and a butterfly.

d) Describe the 4-stage life cycle of moths and butterflies.

e) Why are some caterpillars brightly coloured, when others are camouflaged so that they are very hard to see against their background?

f) Draw a butterfly and label the following parts: head, thorax, abdomen, proboscis, legs, wings, spiracles. What are the proboscis and spiracles used for?

g) Can a butterfly hear?

h) How does a moth navigate?

i) Do moths and butterflies migrate like birds? If so, can you find any examples?

17 *Birds*

a) How are the principles of bird flight the same as those of airplanes and gliders?

b) In small birds the rate of breathing may be 250 times a minute, and the heart may beat 500 times a minute. What is the breathing rate and heart rate of man? Can you explain why they are so different?

c) When a bird breathes, air passes not only into the lungs

but—where? Explain how the bird's system of breathing is very efficient.

d) A bird's vision is very efficient also: find out why, and also how the vision of hawks and owls is very specialized.

e) Birds don't have teeth. How do they chew their food?

f) Describe how birds evolved.

g) Take one of the following types of bird and find out as much as you can about it for a report to the other members of your group:

i) eagle; ii) hawk; iii) hummingbird; iv) penguin; v) owl; vi) cuckoo.

Can you work out the names of the rivers, hills, and mountains marked on the map opposite? To help you, the first letters are given. If you are not sure, look them up in an atlas.

B. Famous People

1 Choose three of the people in each of the lists and find out what they did that was courageous:

a) i) Leonides, King of Sparta
ii) Hannibal
iii) Alfred the Great
iv) Nelson
v) Wolfe of Quebec
vi) William the Silent (of the Netherlands)
vii) Sir Edmund Verney, standard bearer of Charles I
viii) Giuseppe Garibaldi

b) i) Socrates
ii) Simon called Peter
iii) Thomas A Beckett
iv) Joan of Arc
v) Thomas More
vi) Thomas Cranmer
vii) Edmund Campion

c) i) Flora Macdonald
ii) Grace Darling
iii) Marie Curie
iv) Edith Cavell
v) Elizabeth Garrett
vi) Helen Keller
vii) Gladys Aylward

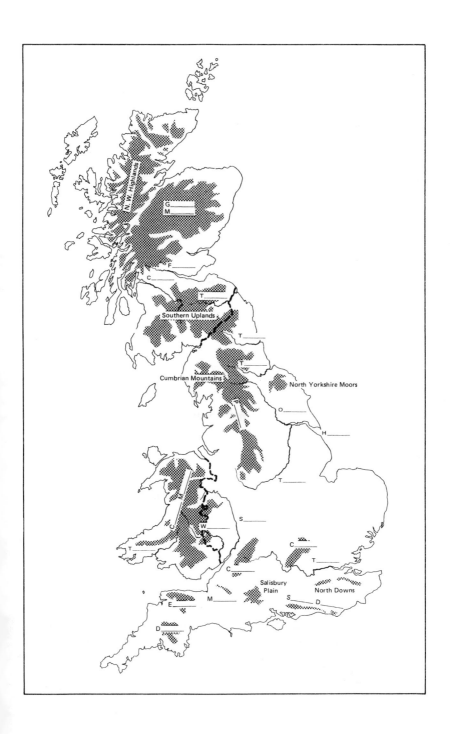

2 *Robert Bruce*

   a) In which year was Robert Bruce crowned King of Scotland? Who was King of England at that time? Were the two countries on friendly terms?

   b) Why did Bruce go into hiding? How did a spider help him to change his mind—and the course of Scottish history?

   c) Give a brief account of what happened at the Battle of Bannockburn.

   d) What happened in 1328 that was important for Bruce, and for Scotland?

   e) How did Bruce die? The intention was that his heart should be buried in Jerusalem, but this didn't take place. Why?

3 *Florence Nightingale*

   a) Why did her parents not agree to her becoming a nurse?

   b) Find out about i) her career before the outbreak of the Crimean War, and ii) why the Crimean War took place, where it happened, and the conditions in which the British soldier had to fight.

   c) Why did she want to go to the Crimea? Did she go alone?

   d) In the Crimea she became known as the Lady of the Lamp—why? Find out as much as you can about what she did there.

e) What happened to her during the rest of her life, after the Crimean War was over?

4   *Thomas Barnardo*
   a) Where was he born, and in which year?
   b) What did he intend to do after training as a doctor?
   c) While training in London, what else did he do?
   d) Who was Jim Jarvis? What did he show Dr Barnardo? What did Dr Barnardo do as the result of what he saw?
   e) Dr Barnardo's work didn't end with the opening of the first home in Stepney in 1870: what did he do after this?

5   *Dick Turpin*
   a) Where did he live and what was his job before becoming a highwayman?
   b) Why did he become a criminal, and what crimes did he commit before working alone as a highwayman?
   c) What did Tom King have to do with his moving to Lincolnshire?
   d) Describe how he came to be arrested.
   e) i) Is it true that he rode non-stop from London to York on Black Bess? If so,
      ii) how long did this famous ride take?

6   *William Kidd* and *Sir Henry Morgan* were both pirates who lived in the 17th century. Both were granted a special favour by a King. Both were arrested and sent for trial: but one was executed, and one was pardoned. Compare the careers of these two men.

7   *Captain William Bligh*
   a) i) What was the name of the ship that Bligh commanded on an expedition to the Pacific Ocean in 1789?
      ii) What was happening in France during that year?
   b) Why did mutiny break out after the ship had left Tahiti? What happened to Bligh?
   c) What was the size of the open boat in which Bligh travelled to Timor? How far was the voyage to Timor? How many companions did Bligh have with him?
   d) How long did it take them to get to Timor? How did they navigate?
   e) What is the connection between Bligh and Captain Cook?

8   *Sir Francis Drake*
   a) In 1555 Drake served in a ship travelling from Africa to
      Spanish settlements in South America: how old was he,
      and what was the ship's cargo?
   b) Later Queen Elizabeth gave him permission to attack
      Spanish ships at sea: describe what happened in one of
      these attacks.
   c) What was the name of the ship in which he sailed around
      the world? How much treasure did he bring back with
      him?
   d) Describe what Drake did to the Spanish fleet i) in Cadiz
      harbour in 1585; ii) in the English Channel in 1588.
   e) What happened to Drake in the remainder of his life?
   f) What is the legend of Drake's drum?
   g) Sir Francis Drake has been called 'brilliantly daring'—
      why?

9   *Christopher Columbus*
   a) i) What did Columbus hope to find by sailing west-
          wards?
      ii) When did he set sail, and where did he sail from?
     iii) How did he manage to afford the ships, sailors, food,
          equipment, etc., for this venture?
   b) What were the names of his flagship and the other ships
      accompanying him on this voyage?
   c) What did he discover during this voyage? When did he
      return to Spain?
   d) Which countries did he discover on subsequent voyages?
      Why did he return to Spain in chains? What happened
      to him when he reached there?
   e) i) What was the purpose of the fourth voyage (1502–4)?
      ii) Did Columbus discover America?

10   *Ferdinand Magellan*
   a) In 1518 Magellan asked King Charles V of Spain for ships
      for a voyage of discovery to—where? What was his plan,
      and why did the King agree to it?
   b) Magellan was a soldier—in which countries had he
      fought, and what wounds had he received?
   c) i) During his voyage Magellan sailed into what had been
          called the South Sea—what was the new name he gave
          it (used to this day), and why did he call it this?
      ii) By this time his fleet had been reduced from five ships
          to three—how?

iii) For ninety-two days the explorers saw no land apart from two desert islands: what did they eat and drink during this time?

d) What happened to the remaining three ships during the rest of this voyage, and to Magellan himself?

e) What was the achievement of this voyage?

11 Find out about one of the following explorers, for a talk to other members of your class or group. Find out about the dangers he faced, and what he discovered.

Marco Polo   Prince Henry the Navigator
Vasco da Gama   Amerigo Vespucci

12 Find out as much as you can about one of the following groups of journeys for a talk to other members of your class or group. Describe the journeys, the difficulties and dangers those taking part had to face, and what you learn about the leaders of the expeditions; and say why you think the journeys were important in the history of exploration:

a) The three voyages of Captain Cook, and the achievement of Baron Bellingshausen in 1819

b) The journeys of William Barents, Henry Hudson, John Franklin, Fridtjof Nansen and Roald Amundsen in the Arctic

c) Expeditions to the Antarctic in 1911, 1914, and 1957

d) The expeditions of Mungo Park, Dr. Livingstone, and Burton and Speke in Africa

Use an atlas to help you find the missing details in the map of Europe on the next page:

Countries: Each number on the map refers to a different country, e.g. 1 = France. Make a list of the numbers 1 to 20 and write the names of the country each number refers to.

Seas and Islands: Each capital letter refers to a sea or an island. Make a list of them — A to I — and write the name of the sea or island each letter refers to, e.g. A = Arctic Ocean.

Cities: Each dot marks a city. The first letter is given e.g. L = London. Can you work out which cities the other dots refer to?

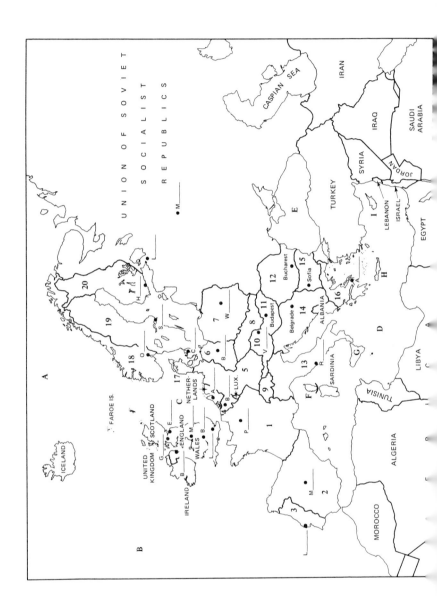

C. Transport

1   *Ships*
    Describe the main changes in the design of ships over the
    centuries, under the following headings:

    a) primitive forms of ships—e.g. ancient Egypt
    b) Viking ships
    c) Changes in ship design from the Middle Ages to the 18th
       century
    d) Sailing ships in 19th century—clippers, whaling ships, etc
    e) Steam ships
    f) Modern ships—oil tankers, submarines, liners, hydro-
       foils.

2   a) How does a ship float?
    b) What is the plimsoll line? What does it do?

3   a) What does a sailor mean when he says 'port' and 'star-
       board'?

    b) Where are the following parts of a ship?
       i) the hull; ii) the bow; iii) the bridge.

    c) What do the following sea terms mean?

       i) abaft; ii) adrift; iii) avast; iv) awash; v) belay; vi)
       clap on; vii) handsomely; viii) shipshape; ix) smack
       it about; x) under way.

4   Find out about ship's time.

a) How is ship's time kept? What are the watches? When do they occur?
b) Two of the watches are called dog watches. When do they occur and how are they different from other watches?
c) Imagine you are a passenger and after lunch you go to your cabin, fall asleep, then wake later in the afternoon to find that your wristwatch has stopped. A bell rings seven times. What is the time?

5   In which year did:

a) Columbus discover the Bahamas?
b) Drake sail from Plymouth on his voyage round the world?
c) The *Mayflower* sail to New England?
d) Captain Cook make his voyage to the Pacific in the *Endeavour*?
e) Nelson lose the sight of his right eye?
f) Nelson lose his right arm?
g) the first steamer cross the Atlantic?
h) the *Titanic* sink?
i) the US submarine Nautilus make the first passage under the North Pole?
j) Sir Francis Chichester i) leave; ii) return to Plymouth after making the first single-handed voyage round the world?

6   Find out about the conditions of service, the discipline, food, living conditions, uniform, and dangers of being a sailor on board a ship in Nelson's fleet.

7   *Trains*

Find out what the following records are:

a) What is the fastest train in the world?
b) What is the longest daily non-stop train journey in the world?
c) What is the world's longest stretch of electrified line?

8   a) Describe how a steam locomotive works.
b) Steam locomotives have largely been replaced today by other types of locomotive—which?
c) Why are these names important in the development of the

steam locomotive? i) James Watt, ii) Trevithick, iii) George Stephenson. Describe what each of these men did that helped in its development.

9   *Isambard Kingdom Brunel*

  a) What work did Brunel do in 1825–28?
  b) What did he design i) in Bristol in 1831; ii) on the Great Western Railway; ii) at Saltash in Cornwall?
  c) He designed three ships—the *Great Western*, the *Great Britain*, and the *Great Eastern*. What was important about each of these ships?

10   *Tunnels*
  a) What is the world's longest tunnel?
  b) Describe how tunnels are made: what happens before drilling starts?
  c) How is the tunnel made through the rock?
  d) How are tunnels made underwater?
  e) List the different uses for tunnels that you can find.

11   *Cars*
  In which year did:
  a) Nicholas Cugnot build a 3-wheeled steam wagon—the first real automobile in the sense that it moved under its own power?
  b) Henry Ford build his first car?
  c) The Rolls Royce Silver Ghost make its first appearance?
  d) The Locomotives Act impose a 4 mph speed limit (2 mph in towns) and require a crew of three for all mechanically propelled vehicles, stipulating that one of the crew must walk not less than 6 yards in front—why?
  e) Two German engineers separately design the prototype of the internal combustion motor car—what were their names?
  f) Malcolm Campbell raise the land speed record above the 300 mph mark for the first time—what was the name of his car?
  g) John Cobb raise the land speed record above the 400 mph mark—where did he do this?
  h) Craig Breedlove raise the land speed record above 600 mph—how was his car propelled?

12   Describe how a) the 2-stroke; b) the 4-stroke petrol engine works; c) what the advantages of a diesel engine are.

13   Explain what these parts of a car do:

i) carburettor; ii) distributor; iii) clutch; iv) gear box; v) radiator.

14   *Air Travel*
Find the dates when these events occurred:

a) Francois Pilatre de Rozier ascended in a hot-air balloon above Paris (how high did he reach?)
b) Louis Bleriot crossed the English Channel in a Bleriot XI monoplane
c) The Royal Air Force was formed
d) Two Australian brothers made the first flight from England to Australia (what were their names, and what was the distance of their flight?)
e) The Australian Flying Doctor service was inaugurated
f) The first solo flight from England to Australia by a woman (what was her name and how long did the journey take?)
g) The first supersonic flight (who was the pilot and what plane did he fly?)
h) Russia put the first earth satellite into orbit (what was it called?)

15   a) All man's early attempts to fly were based on copying the birds. Who was the first to realize that this method is hopeless?
b) How did the following people's inventions help in the development of the airplane:
   i) Sir George Cayley 1804
   ii) W. S. Henson 1843
   iii) Orville Wright 1903
   iv) Alberto Santis-Dumont 1906
   v) Henry Farman, Louis Bleriot 1909
c) Why are these dates and names important in the development of aircraft:
   i) 1919 Alcock and Brown
   ii) 1927 Lindbergh
   iii) Which dates and names during the last 50 years would you add to this list—and why?

16   Amy Johnson
a) i) In 1930 she became the first woman to fly from England to—where?
   ii) What plane did she fly in?

iii) Draw a map to show the stages of her flight—where she started from, where she landed to refuel, and where the journey ended. Can you also find out how long each stage took?

b) Describe the reception given to her on her return to England.

c) She made many more record-breaking flights—give three examples.

d) What did she do in the Second World War?

e) When did she die, and how?

17   a) i) How do aeroplanes fly?

      ii) Why is the wing of an aircraft fairly flat beneath, but curved above?

b) What do 'lift' and 'drag' mean? How do these forces affect the design of aircraft?

c) Why do supersonic planes have delta shape wings?

d) Why is the metal titanium used in some parts of very fast planes, for instance the nose?

18   a) What do these flying terms mean: i) pitch; ii) roll; iii) yaw?

b) i) Explain what happens when the pilot moves the control stick backwards. ii) If you were a pilot how would you make your plane turn left?

19   Find out the different ways in which either a) helicopters or b) jet engines and rockets work.

In the map on the next page each dot marks a city. Can you work out the name?

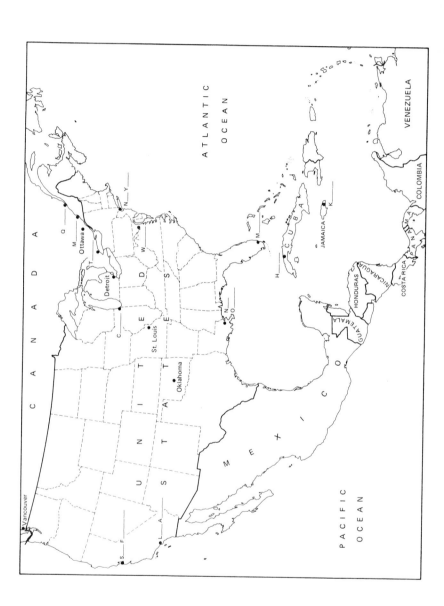

D. Planet Earth

1   a) How far is it to the centre of the earth?
     b) How far is it round the equator?
     c) How far is it from the Earth to the Moon?
     d) How far is it from the Earth to the Sun?

2   a) i) What is the total land area of this planet?
        ii) What is its total water area?
     b) What are the names of the main oceans? Put them in order of size, starting with the smallest and ending with the biggest.
     c) There are six continents. Name them and put them in order of size.

3   a) What is the highest mountain in Europe?
     b) What is the highest mountain in Asia?
     c) What is the highest mountain in Africa?
     d) What is the highest mountain in North America?
     e) What is the highest mountain in South America?

4   a) What is the biggest desert in the world?
     b) What is the biggest lake in the world?
     c) What is the longest river in the world?

5   Here are two lists, one of the names of active volcanoes, one of countries. Match each volcano with the country in which it is found:

Antofalla	Argentina
Beeren Berg	Chile
Asama	Ecuador
Cotopaxi	Iceland
Mount Erebus	Italy
Etna	Aeolian Island, Italy
Hecla	Jan Mayen Island, Greenland Sea
Kluchevskaya	Japan
Nyamuragira	Mexico
Paricutin	New Zealand
Ngauruhoe	Ross Island, Antarctica
Stromboli	Sicily
Vesuvius	USA
Villarica	USSR
Mount Wrangel	Zaire

6   a) How have glaciers affected i) the valleys of the Alps ii) the fjords of Norway iii) the Canadian lakes?
b) How are icebergs formed?
c) How are valleys caused?

7   *Climates*
a)   i) Why are there different climates on Earth?
ii) How would you describe the climate of this country?
b)   Describe the vegetation and animal life of
i) polar climates,
ii) tropical moist climates, and
iii) hot deserts.
c)   Have the climates of the world always been the same?

8   *Clouds*
a) What are clouds? How are they formed?
b) There are different kinds of cloud. Name the types of cloud that:
i) look like curly white wisps of hair drawn out in plumes across a blue sky (the name comes from a Latin word meaning lock of hair) so high in the sky that all the waterdrops are frozen into ice-crystals; what kind of weather do sailors believe this kind of cloud foretells?

    ii) is a layer of low-lying cloud forming an overcast sky from which drizzle falls;

    iii) looks like balls of fleecy white cotton piled into heaps. Why do glider pilots look out for this type of cloud?

    iv) tower up to a far greater height than iii) and are the massive, lowering thunderclouds through which powerful ascending currents carry the cloud to heights where rain, snow and hail are formed.

9   *Monsoons*

  a) The word monsoon comes from the Arabic word *mausim* meaning season.

    i) In which season do monsoons occur and in which parts of the world?

    ii) Why do monsoon rains come at this time?

  b) What kinds of vegetation and animal life are found in monsoon lands?

  c) How do monsoons affect the life of people who live in the lands in which they occur?

10   *Hurricanes*

  a) What is a hurricane? How is it formed?

  b) What is the eye of a hurricane?

  c) i) How can you tell when a hurricane is approaching?

    ii) How long does it last?

    iii) Why does it cause a great deal of damage?

11   *Earthquakes*

  a) i) How many earthquakes are there on average in one year?

    ii) How are they caused?

  b) i) What does a seismograph do?

    ii) How does it work?

  c)   How could earthquakes be controlled?

12   *Oil*

  a) What is oil? How is it discovered?

  b) Describe how oil is taken from the ground, and how it is refined.

  c) How many uses can you list for oil?

  d) In what ways is oil dangerous?

13   *Coal*

  a) What is coal? How did it get into the ground?

b) Describe how coal is extracted from the earth.

c) Why is mining dangerous?
   Describe working conditions in coal mines i) in the early 19th century ii) today.

d) There are coal seams beneath the Antarctic. What does this tell us about the climate of Antarctica in the past?

14   *Cotton*

a) How many uses can you describe for i) cotton lint, ii) cotton seed?

b) When did man start using cotton for clothes?

c) i) In which countries is cotton grown?
    ii) How does the type of cotton grown vary in different countries?
    iii) Explain the different uses that can be made of these varieties of cotton.

d) Describe the process of gathering the cotton and preparing it for weaving into cloth.

15   *Gemstones*

a) Nearly all gemstones are minerals, which normally grow in crystal form.
   i) What do the words 'mineral' and 'crystal' mean?
   ii) How are crystals formed?

b) There are four non-mineral gems. What are they?

c) i) What gives gemstones their colour?
    ii) Gemstones are valued for their 'fire'. What does 'fire' mean?

d) How are diamonds formed?

e) The hardness of a stone (its resistance to scratching) is measured on Mohs' scale which runs from 1 to 10, 10 signifying the hardest minerals. Which number is given for i) diamond, ii) talc, iii) feldspar?

f) What is a lapidary/lapidarist?

16   *Metals*

a) These are used for a great variety of things we need every day: how many different uses can you list?

b) What are the important qualities of metals that make them so useful? (For example, they are hard and strong.)

c) Some things are made out of alternative materials—for instance, glass fibre can be used for car bodywork instead of metal. Can you think of any other examples?

d) What are these metals used for: i) iron, ii) potassium,

iii) silver, iv) gold, v) aluminium, vi) tungsten, vii) mercury, vii) radium, ix) plutonium, x) antimony?
e) What is an alloy? What are the names for these alloys: i) an alloy of copper and tin; ii) an alloy of copper and zinc; iii) what coins are usually made of?
f) Describe what happens in i) smelting, and ii) the casting process.
g) The word metal comes from a Greek word meaning—what?

17 *Electricity*
a) Why does the word 'electricity' come from the Greek word *elektron* which means 'amber'?
b) What is static electricity? How is it caused?
c) What is electric current? How is it measured? What does AC stand for?
d) i) What is an electric circuit? How is it caused?
ii) Describe what happens to the circuit when you switch on and switch off a light switch.
e) i) Where does electricity come from?
ii) An Italian scientist called Luigi Galvani thought it came from frogs' legs—why? What did another Italian scientist Allesandro Volta discover?
f) i) What did the English scientist Michael Faraday discover about the connection between electricity and magnetism?
ii) Why was this discovery very important?
g) Michael Faraday also invented the transformer. Why too was that invention important? What does a transformer do?
h) Fill the gaps in the following passage:
i) The power supply from the power station is —— by transformers from hundreds of thousands of volts to —— volts for household use. Electricity coming into the house passes through a ——. This measures the —— of —— used so that the supplier can —— for it. The current also passes through a ——box. This —— electrical appliances from ——. If too much power is taken the —— —— gets hot and so it ——, breaking the —— and acting as a ——.
ii) Inside the ——s of a petrol engine, a mixture of —— and —— is ignited by electrical —— from a —— ——. The mixture burns and the heat makes it —— pushing down a ——. —— rods and a —— change this up-and-down motion into ——.

18 a) How does a television picture get from a TV camera to your TV set?

b) How does a telephone work?

19 *Isaac Newton*

a) How did an outbreak of plague in Cambridge in 1665 help Isaac Newton's discoveries?

b) Find out about what Newton discovered about i) gravitation, ii) light.

c) Modern telescopes owe a lot to Newton for his inventions: how was the telescope he developed an improvement on earlier models?

d) Shortly before his death Isaac Newton said of himself 'I do not know what I may appear to the world but to myself I have only been a boy playing——.' Can you complete this sentence?

Use an atlas to help you find the missing details on this map of Asia:

Countries: Each number on the map represents a different country, e.g. 1 = Turkey. Make a list of the numbers 1 to 12 and write the name of the country each number refers to.
Seas and Islands: Each capital letter refers to a sea or an island. Make a list of them—A to F—and write the name of the sea or island each letter refers to, e.g. A = Red Sea.

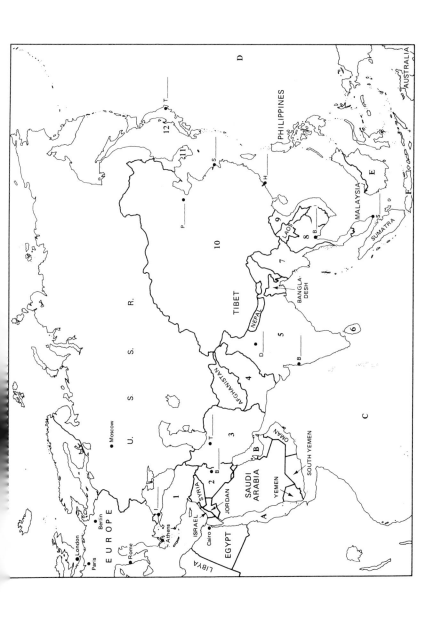

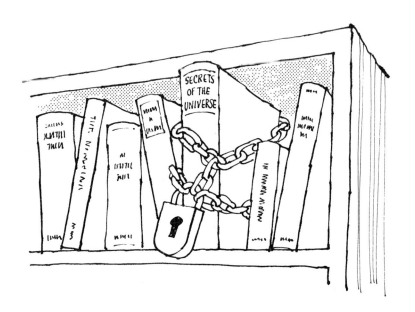

E. The Universe

1   The following paragraphs describe planets in the solar system. Can you identify which planet each paragraph describes?

—— is an average-size star mostly composed of ultra-high-temperature hydrogen and helium. It is more than 109 times the diameter of the Earth, and its mass constitutes more than 99% of the Solar System. The ——'s energy stems from thermonuclear reactions in its core, where hydrogen is converted to helium at very high temperatures and pressures. The temperature of its visible surface is about 6000°C.

—— is small (diameter 4880 km). Its density is high (5.4 g/cc) and it probably has a large iron-rich core with overlying mantle and crust of iron-silicate rocks: the surface is cratered like the Moon's. Surface temperatures range from 500°C at noon to −180°C at night.

——is Earth-like in size (12 104 km in diameter), and with a density of 5.2 g/cc is probably similar in composition and structure. Its atmosphere, largely carbon dioxide, is 100 times as dense as Earth's, so its surface temperature, about 480°C, varies little.

—— is the largest of the 'terrestrial' planets (diameter 12 756 km, density 5.5 g/cc). It is layered, with a dense iron-rich core surrounded by mantle and thin crust of silicate rocks. The crust is seven-tenths covered by water, which, with the atmosphere of oxygen and nitrogen, supports life. Surface temperatures range from 60°C to − 90°C. It has a single large moon.

—— is much smaller than Earth (diameter 6787 km, density 3.9 g/cc), but is also layered into core, mantle and crust. A thin atmosphere mostly consists of carbon dioxide; ice and frozen carbon dioxide form seasonally variable polar icecaps. The apparently lifeless surface is cratered like the Moon but has volcanoes and erosion features. —— has two small moons.

—— are the many thousands of small 'minor planets', most of which orbit the Sun between Mars and Jupiter. Most —— are rocky and less than 10 km across; a few exceed 400 km and the largest (Ceres) is 955 km in diameter. Some —— collision fragments may have been perturbed by Jupiter into orbits that bring them to Earth as meteorites.

—— is the largest planet in the Solar System (diameter 142 800 km), with 14 known moons. It spins rapidly, completing one rotation in under 10 hours. ——'s density is low (1.3 g/cc); a thick atmosphere of hydrogen, helium and ammonia passes down into a planetary body largely composed of liquid and solid hydrogen. The Great Red Spot is a permanent hurricane-like atmospheric storm.

—— is a huge planet (diameter 120 000 km) with ten moons. Its distinctive rings are probably formed by myriads of small ice-covered particles. Like Jupiter, —— consists largely of hydrogen, but has an atmosphere of hydrogen and helium, with some methane: an average piece of —— (density 0.7 g/cc) would float on water.

—— is a large planet (diameter 51 800 km) with five known satellites. Unlike all other planets —— lies on its side, rotating in the plane of its orbit around the Sun. Mostly composed of liquid and solid hydrogen, giving it a density of 1.2 g/cc, —— has an atmosphere of hydrogen, helium and methane which appears greenish in the Sun's reflected light.

—— is smaller than Uranus (diameter 49 500 km) and although more massive (density 1.7 g/cc) is probably similar in composition and structure. Like Uranus it has a slightly green methane-rich atmosphere. It has two moons.

—— is the most enigmatic of the planets. On the assumption that its surface is largely frozen methane, its reflectance of sunlight suggests a diameter of about 3000 km. It takes 248 years to encircle the Sun and its highly elliptical orbit periodically brings it closer to the Sun than Neptune.

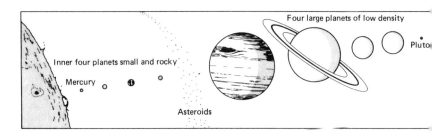

Four large planets of low density

Inner four planets small and rocky

Mercury

Pluto

Asteroids

2   Copy this diagram and label the planets in the solar system.

3   a) Which planet is bigger, Jupiter or Saturn?
    b) On which planets do we know there is life like that on Earth? Why?
    c) At what speed does a meteorite hit the Earth?

4   a) i) How old is the sun?
        ii) How big is it?
        iii) How big is the moon?
    b) What is the Milky Way?
    c) i) What is a galaxy?
        ii) How many can be seen by the naked eye?

5   a) i) What is a star?
        ii) How far away is the nearest star to Earth?
    b) i) What does constellation mean?
        ii) Which is the largest constellation and which is the smallest in the universe?
        iii) How have the constellations helped man for thousands of years?
    c) How many stars are visible to the naked eye on a cloudless night?
    d) Which stars and constellations are most noticeable in the night sky at this season of the year?

6   a) Who was the first to i) make a map of the moon? ii) explain the motion of the moon (in terms of his theory of gravity)? iii) step on the moon?
    b) Why can we be certain that there has never been life on the Moon?
    c) Was the Moon ever joined to the Earth?
    d) How were the craters formed?
    e) How many days does the Moon take to go through its phases, and to orbit round the Earth?

f) What is the connection between the moon and the tides?

g) What is a lunar month? Is it the same as a calendar month?

h) The Moon is constantly turning, rotating on its axis—yet we can never see the far side of the Moon from the Earth. Why?

7   a) Find out the scientific names for the following constellations: i) The Chained Lady ii) The Charioteer, iii) The Herdsman; iv) The Swan; v) The Twins; vi) The Lion; vii) The Winged Horse; viii) The Legendary Hero; ix) The Archer; x) The Scorpion; xi) The Bull; xii) The Great Bear; xiii) The Little Bear.

b) i) What is the speed of light? What is a light year?

c) What do these astronomical terms mean? i) corona; ii) cosmic rays; iii) meteor; iv) scintillation; v) specific gravity; vi) novae; vii) sun-spot; viii) zenith.

8   How do planets keep in their orbits? Why don't they travel on straight lines into space?

Appendixes

1 The Dewey Decimal System— selected subjects and their reference numbers

(Your library may use a simplified version of these numbers, e.g. Acting—792; Cricket—796.)

Acting	792.028
Africa	916/960
Agriculture	630
Aircraft	629.13
Air Transport	387.7
America — North	917/970
— South	918/980
American Civil War	973.7
Animals, wild	590–599
Archaeology	913
Architecture	720–729
Arctic/Antarctic	919.8
Armour	399/739.7
Art	700

-history	709
Astronomy	520
Athletics	796.4
Australia	919.4/994
Aztecs	972
Baby Care	649.1/618.92
Ballet	792.8
Bible	220
Birds	598.2
Botany	581.
Bridges and Roads	388.1/624.2/625
Butterflies	595.789
Canals	386.4
Cars	629.2
Castles	728
Cats	636.8
Churches	726
Cinema	791.43
Coal-mining	622.33
Coin Collecting	737.4
Cookery	641.5
Costume	391
Cricket	796.358
Dams, Reservoirs, etc.	627
Dogs	636.7
Dressmaking	646.4
Egypt, Ancient	932
Electrical Engineering	(e.g. TV) 621
Engineering	620–629
English History	942
Europe	914/940
Flowers	582.13
Farming	630/637
Fishing	639/799.1
Food	641
Football	796.33
Fossils	560
France	914.41/944
Furniture	645.6/749

Gardening	635
Geology	550
Germany	914.3/943
Ghosts	133.1
Greece, Ancient	938
Handicrafts	745.5
The Home and its Equipment	643
Hospitals	362.11
Horses	636.1/798.23
Houses	728
The Human Body	612
Insects	595.7
Islam	297
Japan	915.2/952
Jewellery	739.27
Kites	692.133/796.15
Magic	793.8/133.4
Magic (conjuring)	
Mammals (witchcraft)	599
Manufactures (e.g. leather paper, textiles)	670
Mathematics	510
Medicine	610
Military History	355
Mining	622
Modelmaking	688
Model Aircraft	629.1331
Model Railways	625.19
Model Ships	623.8201
Moslem Religion	297
Motor-cycles	629.227
Motor-racing	796.72
Music	780
Musical Instruments	781.9
Netball	796.31
North America	917/970
Pakistan	915.49/954
Pets	636

Photography	770
Police	363.2
Pop Music	780.42
Ports	387.1
Postal Service	383
Prehistoric Life	560
Railways	625/385
Reptiles	598.1
Roads and Bridges	388.1/624.2/625
Rome, Ancient	937
Scotland	914.1/945
Ships	387.2/623.82
Stamp Collecting	769
Snakes	598.1
South America	918/980
Space Flight	629.4
Sports	796–799
Swimming	797
Tennis	796.342
Trains	385/625
Volcanoes	551.2
Weather	551.4
Wild Flowers	582.13
World War 1	940.3
World War 2	940.53

2 Fiction—have you tried these authors?

Joan Aiken
Nina Bawden
Paul Berna
Lucy M. Boston
Roy Brown
Catherine Cookson
Arthur C. Clarke
Pauline Clarke
John Christopher
Susan Cooper
Meindert Dejong
Peter Dickinson
Penelope Farmer
Nicholas Fisk
Leon Garfield
Alan Garner
John Gordon
Ursula Le Guin
Cynthia Harnett
Rosemary Harris
Clive King
David Line

Joan Lingard
Penelope Lively
Jack London
John Masefield
William Mayne
Bill Naughton
Andre Norton
Phillipa Pearce
K. M. Peyton
Andrew Salkey
Ian Serraillier
Ivan Southall
Rosemary Sutcliff
Geraldine Symons
John Rowe Townsend
Geoffrey Trease
Henry Treece
Kenneth Ullyatt
Jill Paton Walsh
Simon Watson
Laura Ingalls Wilder
Barbara Willard